Superfood Salad Rec...
A Clean Eating Cook...
for Easy Weight Loss a...

by **Vesela Tabakova**
Text copyright(c)2013 Vesela Tabakova

Dedication
To my Wonderful Family, I Love You!

Table Of Contents

Superfoods in Our Backyard	6
My Favorite Superfood Ingredients:	8
Superfood Herbs and Spices in My Recipes	13
Salads with Chicken, Turkey, Beef, Fish or Ham	15
Avocado, Chickpea and Chicken Salad	16
Italian Chicken Salad	17
Balsamic Chicken and White Bean Salad	18
Bulgarian Chicken Salad	19
Chicken and Iceberg Lettuce Salad	20
Quinoa Chicken Salad	21
Chicken and Avocado Salad	22
Chicken, Broccoli and Cashew Salad	23
Greek Chicken Salad	24
Mediterranean Chicken Pasta Salad	25
Chicken and Green Pea Salad	26
Warm Italian Beef and Spinach Salad	27
Beef, Lentil and Walnut Salad	28
Mediterranean Steak Salad	29
Mediterranean Beef Salad	30
Turkey Quinoa Salad	31
Tuna and Green Bean Salad	32
Tuna Salad	33
White Bean and Tuna Salad	34
Beetroot and Carrot Salad with Salmon and Egg	35
Salmon Quinoa Salad Recipe	36
Salmon, Avocado and Asparagus Salad	37
Sausage, Tomatoes and Pasta Salad	38
Potato, Pancetta and Asparagus Salad	39
Shepherds' Salad	40
Fusilli Salad	41
Russian Salad	42
Vegetarian Salads	43
Beet and Bean Sprout Salad	44
Beet Salad with Walnuts	45
Beet Salad with Yogurt	46

Kiwi, Strawberry and Mixed Greens Salad 47
White Bean Salad 48
Warm Quinoa Salad 49
Quinoa and Black Bean Salad 50
Roasted Vegetable Quinoa Salad 51
Quinoa with Oven Roasted Tomatoes and Pesto 52
Cucumber Quinoa Salad 54
Fresh Vegetable Quinoa Salad 55
Warm Mushroom Quinoa Salad 56
Mediterranean Buckwheat Salad 57
Spicy Buckwheat Vegetable Salad 58
Buckwheat Salad with Asparagus and Roasted Peppers 59
Roasted Broccoli Buckwheat Salad 60
Dried Fruit and Feta Cheese Buckwheat Salad 61
Haloumi, Lentil and Rocket Salad 63
Brown Lentil Salad 64
Baby Spinach Salad 65
Tabbouleh 66
Fatoush 67
Greek Salad with Avocado 68
The Best Orzo Salad 69
Blue Cheese Iceberg Salad 71
Apple, Walnut and Radicchio Salad 72
Apple, Celery and Walnut Salad 73
Greek Chickpea Salad 74
Snow White Salad 75
Asian Coleslaw 76
Asian Carrot and Sprout Salad 77
Shredded Egg Salad 78
Fresh Greens Salad 79
Simple Broccoli Salad 80
Caprese Salad 81
Bulgarian Green Salad 82
Green Superfood Salad 83
Fried Zucchinis with Yogurt Sauce 84
Cucumber Salad 85

Tomato Couscous Salad   86
Red Cabbage Salad   87
Cabbage, Carrot and Turnip Salad   88
Carrot Salad   89
Bulgur Salad   90
Roasted Eggplant and Pepper Salad   91
Shopska Salad   92
Okra Salad   93
Green Bean Salad   94
Zucchini Pasta Salad   95
Cheese Stuffed Tomatoes   96
Turkish Spinach Salad   97
Bulgarian Spinach Salad   98
Green Bean and Rocket Salad with Green Olive Dressing   99
Mozzarella, Tomato and Basil Couscous Salad   100
FREE BONUS RECIPES: 10 Natural Homemade Beauty Recipes
that are Easy on the Budget   101
Dry Skin Body Scrub   102
Lavender Body Scrub Recipe   103
Rosemary Body Scrub   104
Banana-Sugar Body Scrub   105
Coffee Body Scrub   106
Strained Yogurt Face Mask   107
Oats Bran Face Mask   108
Pear and Honey Mask   109
Banana Nourishing Mask   110
Apple Autumn Mask   111
About the Author   112

Superfoods in Our Backyard

The foods we eat have an enormous impact on our body and mind. Some foods are really power foods because they not only provide energy to the body but heal and protect it from environmental hazards, aging and illness. The amazing thing I discovered recently is that we actually have plenty of power foods with surprising qualities around us – they are already in our kitchen or backyard. And while some foods get all the glory, recent research has shown that local, common foods we love and eat regularly have the same immunity-boosting, age-defying, fantastic super-powers. These superfoods are inexpensive, quick to cook, delicious, and easy to shop. In fact, most nuts and seeds, dark green vegetables, fatty fish, such as salmon, mackerel and sardines, vegetables with bright, dark or intense colors such as beets and their greens, eggplants, red peppers and tomatoes have potent superfood qualities. Legumes such as peanuts, lentils and beans; citrus fruit and berries, and whole grains are also among the most nutritious foods on the planet. |It is amazing that even the herbs that we grow in our backyards like oregano, basil or rosemary are so chock-full of phytonutrients, antioxidants and vitamins that they have the same healing powers as lots of over the counter medicines.

The reason these foods are frequently called superfoods is that they nourish your body on a very deep level and fight off a range of health disorders. The wonderful effects power foods have on your body can include lowering total cholesterol, regulating blood pressure and helping protect against heart disease or preventing inflammatory processes. Some superfoods are beneficial in fighting cancer cells, while others help protect organs from toxins, promote digestive health, regulate metabolism and burn body fat. If you were to start eating a superfood rich diet today, you would soon see beneficial results. You will boost your immunity, your skin and hair will glow, your nails will grow, your will drop a few pounds and, more importantly, you will feel younger and more energetic.

The salad recipes I have collected for you are all prepared with superfood ingredients and are rich in nutrients that you should be eating every day. They are inexpensive, delicious and easy to prepare.

My Favorite Superfood Ingredients:

Alliums

Leeks, onions, garlic and chives have potent health-enhancing qualities. Research shows that they can help lower blood pressure and cholesterol levels, inhibit the growth of prostate, stomach, and colon cancer cells, and have antibiotic and immune-boosting properties.

Asparagus

Asparagus is very low calorie (only 21 calories in a serving) but is a very good source of folate, vitamin K, vitamins A and C. It is also high in lycopene, a phytonutrient that helps protect cells and other structures in the body from oxygen damage and has cancer-preventing properties. In addition, asparagus is a prebiotic food because it contains inulin, a fiber nourishing to good gut bacteria that line our intestinal tract.

Avocados

Avocados contain the best kind of fats and are extremely good in blocking the absorption of bad fats. Adding them to your diet will aid the body's blood and tissue regeneration, will stabilize blood sugar levels and help prevent heart disorders. In addition to good fats avocados are high in fiber, folate. potassium, vitamin E, and magnesium. They're also high in lutein, which aids eyesight.

Beans

Beans are pretty much the perfect food - high in protein and loaded with fiber, low in cholesterol, and high in folate, iron and magnesium. Eating beans can help lower cholesterol levels and reduce the risk of certain cancers. And because beans are naturally low fat and low calorie, adding them to your diet can cut down the calories without making you feel deprived. Even one of the more calorific bean varieties, contains only 33 calories per ounce.

Beets

The pigment betacyanin, which gives beets their distinctive hue, is just one of several disease-fighting phytonutrients found in this root vegetable. Beets are also a good source of folate, which guards against birth defects, colon cancer, and osteoporosis. They are also high in fiber and beta-carotene.

Broccoli, cabbage, cauliflower

Cruciferous vegetables - cabbages, cauliflower, broccoli contain a powerful range of disease fighting nutrients. They all contain chemicals which have been shown to reduce the risk of lung, colon, breast, ovarian, and bladder cancer. Cruciferous vegetables provide significant cardiovascular benefits as well.

Red cabbage stimulates the immune system, kills bacteria and viruses, and is a good blood purifier. It is rich in anthocyanins which are the same pigment molecules that make blueberries blue and are another powerful antioxidant.

Eating broccoli is great for your hair, skin, and teeth as the vegetable contains more vitamin C than an orange and as much calcium as a glass of milk. It is also a good source of folate which is necessary for the production and maintenance of new cells. Broccoli is also a great source of fiber, potassium, iron and vitamin K. Vitamin K is known to be important for blood coagulation and for maintaining proper bone density. It also plays a key role in the proper development of the fetus.

Buckwheat

While many people think that buckwheat is a cereal grain, it is actually a seed like quinoa. That's why it is a suitable substitute for grains for people with celiac disease, gluten allergies, or anyone trying to avoid gluten. Buckwheat tastes great - nutty and buttery, it is low on the glycemic index, has more protein than rice or wheat and is high in the amino acids lysine and arginine, both of which are essential for a healthy heart and strong immunity. Because it is also high in insoluble fiber, including buckwheat in your menu will help normalize cholesterol levels and reduce hypertension. And there is more: buckwheat has high triptofan levels and will help ensure a sound night's sleep. Magnesium and a natural flavonoid called rutin in buckwheat help to extend the activity of vitamin C and other antioxidant nutrients.

Dark, Leafy Greens

Dark, leafy greens such as spinach, kale, and Swiss chard are incredibly healthy. Low in calories and extremely high in nutrients, they have extraordinarily high levels of antioxidants and are therefore among the best cancer preventing foods. In addition, dark leafy greens are chock-full of vitamins A, C, E and K, Potassium , Magnesium, Iron, Calcium, Folate and many B-vitamins. Dark green leafy vegetables are also very high in fiber, therefore, adding them to your everyday menu is a great way to decrease calories without constantly feeling hungry.

Eggs

Eggs are the best protein source on the planet and outstrip milk, beef, whey, and soy in the quality of protein they provide. They are versatile, economical and nutritious. Egg yolks contain choline, which helps protect heart and brain function, memory, and prevents cholesterol and fat from accumulating in the liver.

Fish

Eating fish helps cut the risk of heart disease, stroke, cancer, Alzheimer's, diabetes, and arthritis. The fatty fish varieties may also help alleviate depression. Wild-caught salmon, herring, and sardines, are the ones that have the most superfood qualities.

Olive Oil

Olive oil is high in monosaturated fat, which has been found to lower blood cholesterol levels, decreasing the risk of heart disease. This type of oil keeps insulin levels low and improves the control of blood sugar. In addition, olive oil contains vitamin K, which aids blood clotting, and vitamin E, an antioxidant important in the creation of red blood cells. The Mediterranean diet, rich in olive oil, creates a lower incidence of heart disease, diabetes, colon cancer, asthma, and atherosclerosis.

Poultry

Poultry is the world's primary source of animal protein. Chicken and turkey offer a rich array of nutrients, particularly niacin, selenium, vitamins B6 and B12, and zinc. These nutrients are essential for a healthy heart and are also valuable in helping lower the risk for cancer.

Tomatoes

Some studies have indicated that incorporating tomatoes in your daily menu may help decrease the risk of prostate cancer, as well as breast, lung and stomach cancers. The reason tomatoes have these miracle qualities is the lycopene – a phytonutrient that has the ability to help protect cells and other structures in the body from oxygen damage and has been proven to have antioxidant and cancer-preventing properties. Lycopene is also good for preventing heart disease. Red tomatoes are the best, because they're packed with more lycopene; and processed tomatoes are just as potent as fresh ones, because it's easier for the body to absorb the lycopene.

Quinoa

Quinoa is the only exotic superfood in my list but I recently fell in love with it and I cannot stop experimenting with different ways to prepare and eat it. It is also one of the healthiest foods on the planet and I think that everyone should give it a try.

Quinoa is a small gluten free seed that is extremely high in protein, fiber, iron, zinc, vitamin E and selenium. It is the only plant-based protein that contains all nine essential amino acids we need for tissue development. These nine essential amino acids are the ones that your body cannot synthesize in quantities sufficient to sustain good health, so they need to come from food sources.

Recent studies have more great news for quinoa eaters. It seems that the processes of boiling, simmering, and steaming quinoa does not significantly compromise the quality of its fatty acids, allowing us to enjoy its cooked texture and flavor while maintaining its nutrient benefits. Food scientists have speculated that it is the diverse array of antioxidants found in quinoa that contribute to this oxidative protection.

Walnuts

Walnuts are rich in fiber, B vitamins, magnesium, selenium, and antioxidants such as Vitamin E. They are also contain more plant sterols and omega-3 fatty acids than any other nuts. Walnuts contain the most alpha-linolenic omega-3 fatty acids, which lower bad cholesterol and may reduce inflammation in arteries.

Yogurt

Like the milk it's made from, yogurt is loaded with calcium, iodine, riboflavin, and vitamin B2. Real yogurt also contains probiotics, the good bacteria your digestive system needs to process and benefit from all the other things you eat and fortify the immune system. Eating yogurt has the added benefit of lowering the bad cholesterol levels and preventing yeast infections.

Superfood Herbs and Spices in My Recipes

The herbs and spices I use in my recipes not only provide natural flavorings to make food more delicious, they are also an incredible source of antioxidants. The superstar herbs are:

Basil

It is a powerful antioxidant that prevents free radical damage, primary cause of heart disease, cancer, and many other serious health conditions, as well as aging. It is an excellent source of vitamin K, calcium, magnesium and beta carotene, manganese, vitamin C and potassium. Basil has amazing anti-inflammatory properties and extraordinary healing benefits that work for arthritis, allergies, and inflammatory bowel conditions.

Dried Red Peppers

Cayenne, crushed red peppers and paprika stimulate digestive enzymes, and help prevent stomach ulcers. Cayenne pepper also reduces bad cholesterol, triglyceride levels, and decreases the formation of harmful blood clots all of which prevent heart attacks and strokes. It is an effective anti-inflammatory and pain relief remedy for everything from headaches to sore muscles, as well as clearing nasal congestion and boosting immunity.

Oregano

It is among the highest in antioxidants of the dried herbs. Its high levels of antioxidants mean that a half teaspoon of dried oregano has the benefits of a spinach salad or three cups of chopped broccoli. Oregano has the added ability to act as an expectorant, clearing congestion, and can also improve digestion.

Rosemary

It contains potent antioxidants and anti-inflammatory agents. The carnosic acid found in rosemary has been shown to reduce stroke risk and shield brain cells from free-radical damage, which can worsen the effects of a stroke. In addition carnosic acid can protect against degenerative diseases like Alzheimer's and other general effects of aging. Adding rosemary to your diet can help improve concentration, boost memory, and lift depression. It can also strengthen the immune system, improve circulation and stimulate digestion.

Salads with Chicken, Turkey, Beef, Fish or Ham

Avocado, Chickpea and Chicken Salad

Serves 4

Ingredients:

1 lb chicken breasts, trimmed

1 cup canned chickpeas, rinsed, drained

1 avocado, halved and thinly sliced

1 cup baby rocket leaves

1 small red onion, halved, thinly sliced

6-7 basil leaves, finely cut

3 tbsp lemon juice

1 garlic clove, crushed

1 tsp cumin

3 tbsp olive oil

Directions:

Place chicken breasts, olive oil and cumin in a dish and toss well to coat. Season with salt and black pepper to taste.

Preheat a barbecue plate or char grill on medium-high heat and cook chicken for five minutes each side or until cooked through. Remove to a plate, cover and set aside for 2-3 minutes to rest. Slice across the grain into 0.5 in thick pieces.

Place chicken pieces, chickpeas, avocado, rocket, onion, and basil in a salad bowl. Mix lemon juice and garlic, then drizzle over salad. Toss to combine and serve.

Italian Chicken Salad

Serves 4

Ingredients:

2 roasted or poached chicken breasts, shredded

2 yellow or orange bell peppers, thinly sliced

1 small red onion, thinly sliced

1 small celery rib, chopped

1/4 cup slivered almonds, toasted

1 tbsp drained capers

juice of one lemon

1 tsp fresh thyme, minced

1/2 cup Parmesan cheese

3 tbsp cup olive oil

1 tbsp mustard

salt and pepper, to taste

Directions:

Combine vegetables and chicken in a salad bowl.

Prepare the dressing by mixing olive oil, lemon juice, mustard, salt and black pepper and drizzle over the salad. Stir well to combine and serve.

Balsamic Chicken and White Bean Salad

Serves 4-6

Ingredients:

1 lb skinless chicken breasts

1 cup canned white beans, drained

1 cup cherry tomatoes, halved

1 cup feta cheese, crumbled

1 cup rocket leaves

2 garlic cloves, crushed

1 tbsp honey

2 tbsp balsamic vinegar

3 tbsp olive oil

Directions:

Whisk garlic, honey and vinegar in a deep bowl. Add chicken breasts and turn to coat. Season with salt and black pepper to taste. Cover and marinate for thirty minutes.

Preheat a barbecue plate or grill on high heat. Lightly brush chicken with oil and cook for two minutes each side or until golden. Reduce heat to medium-low and cook chicken for five minutes each side or until cooked through. Set aside in a plate, covered, for five minutes then slice.

Combine beans, tomatoes, feta cheese, rocket leaves and chicken in a salad bowl. Toss gently and serve.

Bulgarian Chicken Salad

Serves 4-6

Ingredients:

2 cups cooked chicken, chopped

2 hard boiled eggs, diced

2-3 pickled gherkins, chopped

1 large apple, peeled and diced

1/2 cup walnuts, toasted

2 tbsp lemon juice

2 tbsp olive oil

salt and pepper, to taste

Directions:

Bake walnuts in a single layer in a preheated to 400 F oven for three minutes, or until toasted and fragrant, stirring halfway through.

Mix together chicken, apple, eggs and gherkins in a salad bowl.

Combine olive oil and lemon juice, salt and pepper to taste, and add to the chicken mixture. Sprinkle with walnuts and serve.

Chicken and Iceberg Lettuce Salad

Serves 6-7

Ingredients:

2 cups cooked chicken, coarsely chopped

1/2 head iceberg lettuce, halved and chopped

1 celery rib, chopped

1 big apple, peeled and chopped

1/2 red bell pepper, deseeded and chopped

9-10 green olives, pitted and halved

1 red onion, sliced

for the dressing:

2 tbsp olive oil

1 tbsp honey

2 tbsp lemon juice

salt and pepper, to taste

Directions:

Cut all the vegetables and toss them, together with the olives, in a large bowl. Chop the already cooked and cooled chicken into small pieces and add it to the salad.

Prepare the salad dressing in a separate smaller bowl by mixing together the olive oil, honey and lemon juice. Season with salt and pepper, to taste, and serve.

Quinoa Chicken Salad

Serves 6

Ingredients:

1 cup quinoa

2 cups water

2 cups chicken breast, cooked and chopped

1/2 cup black olives, pitted

1 tbsp capers, chopped

1 garlic clove, minced

2 tbsp olive oil

2 tbsp lemon juice

half a bunch fresh parsley, finely cut

salt, to taste

ground black pepper, to taste

Directions:

Wash quinoa in a lot of cold water and cook it according to package directions. Combine olives, capers, garlic, olive oil and lemon juice in a large bowl and stir.

Add in quinoa and mix gently. Stir in chicken and serve.

Chicken and Avocado Salad

Serves 4-6

Ingredients:

2 cups grilled skinless, boneless chicken breast, diced

2 avocados, peeled, pitted and diced

1 red onion, finely chopped

1/2 cup green olives, pitted

10 cherry tomatoes

2 tbsp lemon juice

3 tbsp olive oil

1 tsp oregano

salt and black pepper to taste

Directions:

In a medium bowl, combine the avocados, chicken, onion, and cherry tomatoes. Season with oregano, salt and pepper to taste.

Add the olives, lemon juice and olive oil and toss lightly to coat.

Chicken, Broccoli and Cashew Salad

Serves 6

Ingredients:

1 lb fresh broccoli, cut in florets

1 cup grilled boneless chicken breast, diced

3.5 oz cashews, baked

3.5 oz sunflower seeds, salted and baked

2 tbsp Parmesan cheese, grated

1/2 cup fresh parsley leaves, finely cut

2 tbsp olive oil

2 tbsp lemon juice

Directions:

Wash broccoli and steam it for five minutes until just tender.

Transfer broccoli into a large salad bowl and leave it to cool then mix it with the chicken pieces. Add in cashews, sunflower seeds and the finely cut parsley.

In a smaller cup, mix the olive oil and lemon juice. Pour over the salad and serve sprinkled with Parmesan cheese.

Greek Chicken Salad

Serves 4

Ingredients:

4 small chicken breasts

1/3 cup lemon juice

1-2 tsp chopped fresh rosemary

3 garlic cloves, crushed

1/4 cup olive oil

2 tomatoes, cut into thin wedges

1 small red onion, cut into thin wedges

1/4 cup black olives

3.5 oz feta, crumbled

1/4 cup parsley leaves, chopped

Directions:

Prepare the dressing from the lemon juice, garlic, rosemary and olive oil. Place chicken breasts in a bowl with half the dressing. Stir well and marinate for at least fifteen minutes.

Heat a grill pan or non-stick frying pan over medium high heat. Cook the chicken for five minutes each side until golden and cooked through. Set aside, covered with foil.

Toss the tomatoes, onion, olives, feta and parsley in the remaining dressing. Slice the chicken thickly and add to the salad, then toss gently to combine.

Mediterranean Chicken Pasta Salad

Serves 6-8

Ingredients:

3 cups medium wholewheat pasta, cooked

1 small roasted chicken, skin and bones removed, shredded

1 cup cherry tomatoes

1 cucumber, halved, sliced

1 red bell pepper, sliced

1 small red onion, sliced

1/3 cup fresh basil leaves, finely chopped

1/3 cup parsley leaves, finely chopped

1 cup black olives, pitted

1/3 cup pine nuts, toasted

for the dressing

1/3 cup red wine vinegar

1/4 cup olive oil

1 garlic clove, crushed

Directions:

Place pasta, chicken, tomato, cucumber, bell pepper, onion, basil, parsley, olives and pine nuts in a large bowl.

Make the dressing by combining vinegar, oil, garlic and salt. Pour the dressing over the salad and toss to combine.

Chicken and Green Pea Salad

Serves 4

Ingredients:

2 cups chicken breast, cooked and chopped

1 cup green peas, cooked or from a can

1 medium apple, diced

1 garlic clove, minced

2-3 green onions, finely cut

a bunch of fresh dill, finely cut

salt and ground black pepper to taste

2 tbsp lemon juice

2 tbsp olive oil

Directions:

Combine all salad ingredients in a bowl and mix well. Serve chilled.

Warm Italian Beef and Spinach Salad

Serves 6

Ingredients:

8 oz deli Italian roast beef, cut into 1/ 4 inch strips

1 red onion, sliced and separated into rings

2 tomatoes, sliced

1 red pepper, sliced

6 cups baby spinach leaves or fresh spinach, torn

2 tbsp olive oil

1/2 cup grated Parmesan cheese, to serve

for the dressing:

1/2 cup sour cream

1 tbsp mustard

2 garlic cloves, crushed

Directions:

Stir together all dressing ingredients in a deep bowl and set aside.

Warm olive oil in a large skillet and sauté beef and onions. Cook for three minutes, stirring occasionally, over medium heat until beef is heated through.

Toss together beef, spinach, tomatoes, red pepper and dressing in a large salad bowl. Serve sprinkled with Parmesan cheese.

Beef, Lentil and Walnut Salad

Serves 6

Ingredients:

4 beef fillet steaks

1/3 cup olive oil

1 can lentils, rinsed and drained

1 bunch radishes, trimmed and thinly sliced

1/2 cup black olives, pitted

1 cup baby spinach leaves

1/2 cups walnuts, halved and toasted

2-3 green onions, chopped

1/4 cup red wine vinegar

1/2 tsp cumin

salt and black pepper to taste

Directions:

Preheat a barbecue grill or char grill on medium-high heat. Brush steaks with olive oil. Season with salt and pepper to taste and cook for 3-4 minutes each side for medium or until cooked to your liking. Transfer to a plate, cover and set aside.

Put lentils, radishes, walnuts, green onions and baby spinach in a salad bowl. Prepare the dressing by mixing the remaining olive oil, red wine vinegar and cumin. Drizzle dressing over lentils mixture and toss to combine. Slice beef steaks and add to the salad.

Mediterranean Steak Salad

Serves 4

Ingredients:

1 lb boneless beef sirloin steak, about 1 inch thick

4 cups, romaine or rocket leaves

1 red onion, sliced and separated into rings

1 cup cherry tomatoes, halved

1/2 cup green olives, pitted

1/2 feta cheese, crumbled

1 tsp salt

1/2 tsp black pepper

for the dressing:

3 garlic cloves, crushed

5 tbsp olive oil

5 tbsp lemon juice

1 tsp lemon zest

1/2 tsp dried thyme

Directions:

Prepare the dressing by combining all ingredients in a bowl.

Heat a heavy skillet. Season steak with salt and ground black pepper. Cook it for 3-4 minutes on medium heat then turn it and cook for 3-4 minutes more. Transfer steak to a cutting board and leave it to cool. Slice it thinly.

Divide romaine lettuce among four plates. Top with sliced meat, red onion, tomatoes, olives and feta cheese. Drizzle with dressing.

Mediterranean Beef Salad

Serves 4

Ingredients:

8 oz roast beef, thinly sliced

6 cups mixed greens, torn

1 cucumber, cut

6-7 fresh mushrooms, thinly sliced

4 tbsp fresh basil leaves, torn

2 tbsp balsamic vinegar

4 tbsp olive oil

1 tsp salt

Directions:

Prepare the dressing by mixing vinegar, olive oil, crushed garlic, salt and basil leaves in a bowl.

Divide greens among four plates. Arrange beef with cucumbers and mushrooms on top. Drizzle with dressing.

Turkey Quinoa Salad

Serves 6

Ingredients:

1 cup quinoa

2 cups water

1 cup skinless lean turkey breast, cooked, diced

1 small red onion, chopped

2 carrots, diced and cooked

1 cup green peas, cooked

2 tbsp olive oil

1 tbsp lemon juice

salt and black pepper, to taste

Directions:

Wash quinoa with lots of water. Strain it and cook it according to package directions. When ready, set aside in a large salad bowl and fluff with a fork.

Add in the turkey, onion, carrots and green peas. Combine oil, lemon juice, salt and pepper in a separate bowl and stir until well mixed.

Pour dressing over quinoa mixture and stir again. Cover and chill until ready to serve.

Tuna and Green Bean Salad

Serves 4

Ingredients:

1 cup medium whole wheat pasta

9 oz green beans, trimmed and cut into 2 in lengths

1 cup cherry tomatoes, halved

1 ripe avocado, peeled and cubed

1 can tuna, drained and broken into big chunks

1/4 cup olive oil

2 tbsp lemon juice

2 tsp mustard

Directions:

Cook pasta in boiling water for 10 minutes. Add the green beans and cook for 4 more minutes. Drain and cool.

Prepare the dressing by combining together olive oil, lemon juice and mustard. Season with salt and black pepper to taste.

Combine pasta, beans, cherry tomatoes, avocado, tuna and the dressing. Toss gently and serve.

Tuna Salad

Serves 4

Ingredients:

1 head green lettuce, washed and drained

1 cucumber, peeled and cut

1 can tuna, drained and broken into big chunks

1/2 cup sweet corn, from a can

a bunch of radishes

a bunch of green onions

juice of half lemon or 2 tbsp of white wine vinegar

3 tbsp olive oil

salt, to taste

Directions:

Cut the lettuce into thin strips. Slice the cucumber and the radishes as thinly as possible and chop the spring onions.

Combine all vegetables in a large bowl, add the tuna and the sweet corn and season with lemon juice, oil and salt to taste.

White Bean and Tuna Salad

Serves 4

Ingredients:

2 cups canned white beans, rinsed and drained

1 cup canned tuna, drained and broken into chunks

1 red onion, sliced

1/2 cup black olives, pitted and halved

juice of one lemon

1/2 cup fresh parsley leaves, chopped

1 tsp dried mint

salt and freshly ground black pepper, to taste

3 tbsp olive oil

Directions:

Put tuna chunks in a large bowl. Add the beans and gently stir to combine.

Add olives, onions, parsley, mint, lemon juice and olive oil and mix to combine. Season with salt and black pepper to taste. Serve chilled.

Beetroot and Carrot Salad with Salmon and Egg

Serves 4

Ingredients:

3 eggs, boiled and quartered

2 beets, peeled and coarsely grated

2 carrots, peeled and coarsely grated

5 oz smoked salmon, flaked

3-4 green onions, chopped

1 tsp chia seeds

1/4 cup fresh lemon juice

2 tbsp olive oil

salt and black pepper, to taste

Directions:

Boil eggs over high heat for 5 minutes. Drain, cool and peel. Shred carrots and beets and divide them among serving plates. Cut each egg in quarters and place on top of the vegetables. Top with the salmon flakes.

Prepare the dressing by whisking lemon juice and oil in a small bowl. Season with salt and pepper and drizzle the dressing over the salad. Serve sprinkled with green onions.

Salmon Quinoa Salad Recipe

Serves 6-7

Ingredients:

1 cup quinoa

2 cups water

1 cup canned salmon pieces

1 red pepper, cut into strips

1/2 cup canned sweet corn, drained

1 tsp mustard

1 tsp lemon juice

1 bunch green onions, chopped

3 tbsp fresh parsley leaves, finely cut

1 tbsp fresh dill, finely cut

freshly ground black pepper, to taste

Directions:

Rinse quinoa in a fine sieve under cold running water until water runs clear. Put quinoa in a pot with two cups of water. Bring to a boil, then reduce heat, cover and simmer for fifteen minutes or until water is absorbed and quinoa is tender. Fluff quinoa with a fork and set aside to cool.

In a large bowl mix the salmon, corn, red pepper, mustard and lemon juice. Mix in the green onions, parsley and dill.

Stir in the cooked quinoa. Season with freshly ground pepper to taste. Serve chilled.

Salmon, Avocado and Asparagus Salad

Serves 4

Ingredients:

1 cucumber, peeled and chopped

1 avocado, peeled and cubed

1 bunch asparagus, trimmed, cut into 2 in lengths

1/2 cup soy sprouts, trimmed

1 can salmon, drained and broken into large chunks

2 tbsp light sour cream

1 tbsp lemon juice

1 tbsp dill, very finely chopped

Directions:

Cook asparagus in boiling salted water for 1-2 minutes or until bright green and tender. Drain and rinse and pat dry.

Place asparagus, cucumber, avocado, soy sprouts and salmon into a salad bowl.

Toss well to combine. Prepare the dressing by whisking together sour cream and lemon juice. Season with salt and pepper to taste. Drizzle salad with dressing and sprinkle with dill.

Sausage, Tomatoes and Pasta Salad

Serves 6-8

Ingredients:

1 cup whole wheat spiral pasta

2 tbsp olive oil

1 lb pork sausages

2 zucchinis, sliced lengthwise

1 1/2 cups cherry tomatoes

1 cup small mozzarella cheese, sliced

4 tbsp olive oil

4 tbsp lemon juice

1 tsp dried basil

Directions:

Cook pasta following package directions, until al dente. Drain and transfer to a bowl. Stir in two tablespoons of olive oil. Set aside to cool.

Grill sausages, turning, for 10 minutes or until just cooked through. Set aside to cool slightly and slice thickly. Grill zucchinis, until char-grilled. Transfer to a plate. Grill tomatoes for 1 minute.

Combine sausages, zucchinis, tomatoes and mozzarella with pasta. Prepare the dressing by combining lemon juice, olive oil and basil. Drizzle over salad and stir. Season with salt and pepper and toss to combine. Serve warm.

Potato, Pancetta and Asparagus Salad

Serves 6

Ingredients:

2 lbs spring potatoes, washed, peeled, halved lengthwise

4 tbsp olive oil

2 garlic cloves, crushed

6 slices mild pancetta

1 bunch asparagus, trimmed and cut diagonally into 2 inch lengths

1/2 cup green beans, cut into 2 inch lengths

1 tbsp red wine vinegar

2 tbsp olive oil

1 tbsp mustard

a bunch of green onions, finely cut

Directions:

Preheat oven to 350 F. Combine potatoes, olive oil and garlic in a large baking dish. Season with salt and pepper to taste and bake turning occasionally, for about 20 minutes, or until golden brown.

Heat a large frying pan over medium heat. Cook the pancetta slices for 1 minute each side or until crisp. Drain and transfer to a plate. Cook the asparagus and green beans in salted boiling water for 3 minutes or until bright green and tender crisp. Drain.

Break the pancetta into large pieces. Place in a large serving bowl along with the potatoes, asparagus, green beans and green onions.

Combine the remaining oil, vinegar and mustard in a small bowl. Season with salt and pepper and pour over the salad. Gently toss and serve.

Shepherds' Salad

Serves 6-8

Ingredients:

5-6 tomatoes, sliced

2 cucumbers, peeled and sliced

5-6 white mushrooms, sliced

2 red bell peppers, sliced

7 oz ham, diced

1 onion, sliced

3 eggs, boiled and sliced

7 oz feta cheese, grated

1/2 bunch parsley, finely cut

4 tbsp olive oil

1 tbsp red wine vinegar

1 tsp salt

20-30 black olives

Directions:

Slice the tomatoes, cut the cucumbers, peppers and onion, thinly slice the mushrooms. Dice the ham.

Combine all ingredients in a salad bowl and drizzle with olive oil and vinegar. Season with salt and mix well.

Divide the salad in plates and sprinkle with feta cheese and parsley. Top with egg slices and olives. Serve chilled.

Fusilli Salad

Serves 6

Ingredients:

2 cups fusilli pasta

1 onion, chopped

1 green bell pepper, chopped

2 tomatoes, chopped

1 cup mushrooms, sliced

7 oz ham, cut

3 tbsp lemon juice

3 tbsp olive oil

Directions:

Cook pasta according to package directions or until al dente then rinse under cold water and drain.

In a large bowl combine pasta, onion, bell pepper, tomatoes, mushrooms and ham. Prepare the dressing from olive oil and lemon juice together with salt and pepper to taste.

Pour the dressing over the salad, toss and serve chilled.

Russian Salad

Serves 6

Ingredients:

3 potatoes, boiled, cut in small cubes

2 carrots, boiled, cut in small cubes

1 cup canned green peas, drained

6 oz ham, cut in cubes

1 cup homemade mayonnaise

5 pickled gherkins, chopped

salt to taste

Directions:

Boil the potatoes and carrots, then chop into small cubes.

Put all ingredients in a salad bowl and mix with a spoon. Add salt to taste, stir and serve.

Vegetarian Salads

Beet and Bean Sprout Salad

Serves 4-6

Ingredients:

7 beet greens, finely sliced

2 medium tomatoes, cut into wedges

1 cup bean sprouts, washed

1 tbsp grated lemon rind

2 garlic cloves, crushed

4 tbsp cup lemon juice

4 tbsp olive oil

1 tsp salt

Directions:

In a large salad bowl toss together beet greens, bean sprouts and tomatoes.

Prepare a dressing from the oil, lemon juice, lemon rind, salt and garlic and pour it over the salad. Set aside in the fridge and serve chilled.

Beet Salad with Walnuts

Serves 4

Ingredients:

3 medium beets, steamed and diced

1 onion, sliced

1/2 cup walnut halves

1 tsp lemon juice

1 tbsp olive oil

4-5 mint leaves

½ tsp salt

Directions:

Wash beets well, cut the stems, and steam in a pot until cooked through.

Let them cool down, then peel and dry them. Cut beets and place them in a salad bowl.

Add the walnuts, onion, lemon juice and olive oil and toss. Serve cold, sprinkled with fresh mint leaves.

Beet Salad with Yogurt

Serves 4

Ingredients:

3 medium beets

1 cup strained yogurt

2 garlic cloves, crushed

1 tsp white wine vine vinegar or lemon juice

1 tbsp olive oil

1/2 tsp dried mint

½ tsp salt

Directions:

Wash beets, cut the stems and steam them in a pot for 25-30 minutes, or until cooked through.

When they cool down, peel and dry with a paper towel then grate and place them in a deep salad bowl.

Add the other ingredients and toss. Serve cold.

Kiwi, Strawberry and Mixed Greens Salad

Serves 4

Ingredients:

2 kiwis, cubed

6-7 medium strawberries, halved

2 cups mixed greens

1/2 cup croûtons

for the dressing

1/2 cup orange juice

4 tbsp olive oil

1 tbsp balsamic vinegar

1/2 tsp salt

Directions:

Prepare the dressing by whisking together orange juice, olive oil, balsamic vinegar and salt.

Cut the strawberries and kiwis. Arrange the mixed greens in a salad bowl and toss in the dressing. Add strawberries and kiwis on top and serve sprinkled with croûtons.

White Bean Salad

Serves 4-5

Ingredients:

1 cup dry white beans

1 onion, whole

1/2 onion, chopped

3 red wine vinegar

a bunch of fresh parsley

salt and black pepper

1 tsp fresh mint

Directions:

Wash the beans and soak them in cold water to swell overnight. Cook in the same water with the peeled onion. When tender, drain and put into a deeper bowl. Remove the onion.

Mix well oil, vinegar, salt and pepper. Pour over still warm beans, leave to cool about 30-40 minutes.

Chop the onion and the mint, add to the beans, mix and leave to cool for at least 40 minutes. Serve cold.

Warm Quinoa Salad

Serves 6

Ingredients:

1 cup quinoa

2 cups water

1/2 cup green beans, frozen

1/2 cup sweet corn, frozen

1/2 cup carrots, diced

1/2 cup black olives, pitted

2 garlic cloves, crushed

2 tbsp soy sauce

2 tbsp fresh dill, finely cut

3 tbsp lemon juice

2 tbsp olive oil

Directions:

Wash quinoa with lots of water. Strain it and cook it according to package directions. When ready set aside in a large salad bowl.

Stew green beans, sweet corn and carrots in a little olive oil until tender. Add to quinoa.

In a smaller bowl, combine soy sauce, lemon juice, dill and garlic and pour over the warm salad. Add salt and pepper to taste and serve.

Quinoa and Black Bean Salad

Serves 6

Ingredients:

1 cup quinoa

1 cup black beans, cooked, rinsed and drained

1/2 cup sweet corn, cooked

1 red bell pepper, deseeded and chopped

4 spring onions, chopped

1 garlic clove, crushed

1 tbsp dry mint

2 tbsp lemon juice

1/2 tsp salt

1 tbsp apple cider vinegar

4 tbsp cup olive oil

Directions:

Rinse quinoa in a fine sieve under cold running water until water runs clear. Put quinoa in a pot with two cups of water.

Bring to a boil, then reduce heat, cover and simmer for fifteen minutes or until water is absorbed and quinoa is tender. Fluff quinoa with a fork and set aside to cool.

Put beans, corn, bell pepper, spring onions and garlic in a bowl and toss with vinegar and black pepper to taste. Add quinoa and toss well again.

In a separate bowl whisk together lemon juice, salt and olive oil and drizzle over salad. Toss well and serve.

Roasted Vegetable Quinoa Salad

Serves 6

Ingredients:

2 zucchinis, cut into bite sized pieces

1 eggplant cut into bite sized pieces

3 roasted red peppers, cut into bite sized pieces

4-5 small white mushrooms, whole

1 cup quinoa

1/2 cup olive oil

1 tbsp apple cider vinegar

1/2 tsp savory

salt and pepper to taste

7 oz feta, crumbled

Directions:

Toss the zucchinis, mushrooms and eggplant in half the olive oil, salt and pepper. Place onto a baking sheet in a single layer and bake in a preheated 350 F oven for 30 minutes flipping once.

Wash well, strain and cook the quinoa following package directions.

Prepare the dressing from the remaining olive oil, apple cider vinegar, savory, salt and pepper.

In a big bowl combine quinoa, roasted zucchinis, eggplant mushrooms, roasted red peppers, and feta. Toss the dressing into the salad.

Quinoa with Oven Roasted Tomatoes and Pesto

Serves 6

Ingredients :

for the salad

1 cup dry quinoa

2 cups water

1 cup cherry tomatoes, for roasting

1/2 cup cherry tomatoes, fresh

1 avocado, cut into chunks

1/2 cup black olives, pitted

1 cup mozzarella cheese, cut into bite size pieces

for the pesto

1 clove garlic, chopped

1/2 tsp salt

1/2 cup walnuts, toasted

1 cup basil leaves

1 tbsp lemon juice

1 tbsp mustard

4-6 tbsp olive oil

1 tsp savory

2 tbsp water (optional)

Directions:

Preheat the oven to 350 F. Line a baking sheet with foil. Make sure the tomatoes are completely dry, then drizzle with olive oil and savory and toss to coat them all.

Bake the tomatoes for about twenty minutes, flipping once, until they are brown. Sprinkle with salt.

Rinse quinoa very well in a fine sieve under running water; set aside to drain. Place two cups of water and quinoa in a large saucepan over medium-high heat. Bring to the boil then reduce heat to low. Simmer for fifteen minutes. Set aside, covered, for ten minutes and fluff with a fork.

Make the pesto by placing garlic, walnuts and 1/2 teaspoon salt in a food processor. Add basil, mustard and lemon juice and blend in batches until smooth. Add oil, one tablespoon at a time, processing in between, until the pesto is lightened and creamy. For an even lighter texture you can add two tablespoons of water. Taste for salt and add more if you like.

In a large mixing bowl, gently mix the quinoa with the tomatoes, avocado, olives and mozzarella pieces. Spoon in the pesto and toss to distribute it evenly.

Cucumber Quinoa Salad

Serves 6

Ingredients:

1 cup quinoa, rinsed

2 cups water

1 large cucumber, diced

1/2 cup black olives, pitted

2 tbsp lemon juice

2 tbsp olive oil

1 bunch fresh dill, finely cut

Directions:

Wash quinoa very well in a fine mesh strainer under running water and set aside to drain. Place quinoa and two cups of cold water in a saucepan over high heat and bring to the boil. Reduce heat to low and simmer for fifteen minutes. Set aside, covered, for ten minutes, then transfer to a large bowl.

Add finely cut dill, cucumber and olives. Prepare a dressing from the lemon juice, olive oil, salt and pepper. Add it to the salad and toss to combine.

Fresh Vegetable Quinoa Salad

Serves 6

Ingredients:

1 cup quinoa

2 cups water

a bunch of fresh onions, chopped

2 green peppers, chopped

1/2 cup black olives, pitted and chopped

2 tomatoes, diced

1 cup raw sunflower seeds

3 tbsp olive oil

4 tbsp fresh lemon juice

1 tbsp dried mint

Directions:

Prepare the dressing by combining olive oil, lemon juice, and dried mint in a small bowl and mixing it well. Place the dressing in the refrigerator until ready to use.

Wash well and cook quinoa according to package directions. When it is ready leave it aside for ten minutes, then transfer it to a large bowl.

Add the diced peppers, finely cut fresh onions, olives and diced tomatoes stirring until mixed well. Stir the dressing (it will have separated by this point) and add it to the salad, tossing to evenly coat. Add salt and pepper to taste and sprinkle with sunflower seeds.

Warm Mushroom Quinoa Salad

Serves 4-5

Ingredients:

1 cup quinoa

2 cups vegetable broth

1 tbsp sunflower oil

2-3 spring onions, chopped

2 garlic cloves, chopped

10 white mushrooms, sliced

1-2 springs of fresh rosemary

1/2 cup dried tomatoes, chopped

2 tbsp olive oil

salt and freshly ground pepper

1/2 bunch fresh parsley

Directions:

Wash well the quinoa in plenty of cold water, strain it and put it in a saucepan. Add vegetable broth and bring to the boil. Lower heat and simmer for ten minutes until the broth is absorbed.

Heat oil in a frying pan and sauté onions for 2-3 minutes. Add garlic and sauté for another minute. Add sliced mushrooms and season with salt and pepper. Finally, add the rosemary. Stir fry the mushrooms until soft.

Mix well the cooked quinoa with the mushrooms and tomatoes. Serve sprinkled with fresh parsley.

Mediterranean Buckwheat Salad

Serves 4-5

Ingredients:

1 cup buckwheat groats

1 3/4 cups water

1 small red onion, finely chopped

1/2 cucumber, diced

1 cup cherry tomatoes, halved

1 yellow bell pepper, chopped

a bunch parsley, finely cut

1 preserved lemon, finely chopped

1 cup chickpeas, cooked or canned, drained

juice of half lemon

1 tsp dried basil

2 tbsp olive oil

Directions:

Heat a large, dry saucepan and toast the buckwheat for about three minutes. Boil the water and add it carefully to the buckwheat. Cover, reduce heat and simmer until buckwheat is tender and all liquid is absorbed (5-7 minutes). Remove from heat, fluff with a fork and set aside to cool.

Mix the buckwheat with the chopped onion, bell pepper, cucumber, cherry tomatoes, parsley, preserved lemon and chickpeas in a salad bowl.

Whisk the lemon juice, olive oil and basil, season with salt and pepper to taste, then pour over the salad and stir.

Spicy Buckwheat Vegetable Salad

Serves 4-5

Ingredients:

1 cup buckwheat groats

2 cups vegetable broth

2 tomatoes, diced

1/2 cup spring onions, chopped

1/2 cup parsley leaves, finely chopped

1/2 cup fresh mint leaves, very finely chopped

1/2 yellow bell pepper, chopped

1 cucumber, peeled and cut into 1/4-inch cubes

1/2 cup cooked or canned brown lentils, drained

1/4 cup freshly squeezed lemon juice

1 tsp hot pepper sauce

salt, to taste

Directions:

Heat a large, dry saucepan and toast the buckwheat for about three minutes. Boil the vegetable broth and add it carefully to the buckwheat. Cover, reduce heat and simmer until buckwheat is tender and all liquid is absorbed (five-seven minutes). Remove from heat, fluff with a fork and set aside to cool.

Chop all vegetables and add them together with the lentils to the buckwheat. Mix the lemon juice and remaining ingredients well and drizzle over the buckwheat mixture. Stir well to distribute the dressing evenly.

Buckwheat Salad with Asparagus and Roasted Peppers

Serves 4-5

Ingredients:

1 cup buckwheat groats

1 3/4 cups vegetable broth

1/2 lb asparagus, trimmed and cut into 1 in pieces

4 roasted red bell peppers, diced

2-3 spring onions, finely chopped

2 garlic cloves, crushed

1 tbsp red wine vinegar

3 tbsp olive oil

salt and black pepper, to taste

1/2 cup fresh parsley leaves, finely cut

Directions:

Heat a large, dry saucepan and toast the buckwheat for about three minutes. Boil the vegetable broth and add it carefully to the buckwheat. Cover, reduce heat and simmer until buckwheat is tender and all liquid is absorbed (five-seven minutes). Remove from heat, fluff with a fork and set aside to cool.

Rinse out the saucepan and then bring about an inch of water to a boil. Cook the asparagus in a steamer basket or colander, two to three minutes until tender. Transfer the asparagus in a large bowl along with the roasted peppers.

Add in the spring onions, garlic, red wine vinegar, salt, pepper and olive oil. Stir to combine. Add the buckwheat to the vegetable mixture. Sprinkle with parsley and toss the salad gently. Serve at room temperature.

Roasted Broccoli Buckwheat Salad

Serves 4-5

Ingredients:

1 cup buckwheat groats

1 3/4 cups water

1 head of broccoli, cut into small pieces

1 lb asparagus, trimmed and cut into 1 in pieces

1/2 cup roasted cashews

1/2 cup basil leaves, minced

1/2 cup olive oil

2 garlic cloves, crushed

1 tsp salt

3 tbsp Parmesan cheese, grated, to serve

Directions:

Arrange vegetables on a baking sheet and drizzle with olive oil. Roast in a preheated to 350 F oven for about fifteen minutes or until tender.

Heat a large, dry saucepan and toast the buckwheat for about three minutes, or until it releases a nutty aroma. Boil the water and add it carefully to the buckwheat. Cover, reduce heat and simmer until buckwheat is tender and all liquid is absorbed (five-seven minutes). Remove from heat, fluff with a fork and set aside to cool.

Prepare the dressing by blending basil leaves, olive oil, garlic, and salt.

Toss vegetables, buckwheat and dressing together in a salad bowl. Add in cashews and serve sprinkled with Parmesan cheese.

Dried Fruit and Feta Cheese Buckwheat Salad

Serves 4

Ingredients:

1 cup buckwheat groats

1 3/4 cups water

1 celery rib, finely chopped

1 large endive, shredded

1/2 cup roasted walnuts, chopped

1/2 cup dried apricots, chopped

1/2 cup dried prunes, chopped

1/2 cup raisins

juice of half orange

1 tbsp balsamic vinegar

2 tbsp fresh mint, finely chopped

1/2 tsp salt

1/2 tsp black pepper

1 tbsp olive oil

3 oz feta cheese, crumbled

Directions:

Heat a large, dry saucepan and toast the buckwheat for about three minutes, or until it releases a nutty aroma. Boil the water and add it carefully to the buckwheat. Cover, reduce heat and simmer until buckwheat is tender and all liquid is absorbed (five-seven minutes).

Remove from heat, fluff with a fork and set aside to cool.

Combine dried fruit, buckwheat and all other ingredients in a large salad bowl. Toss to mix well and serve immediately.

Haloumi, Lentil and Rocket Salad

Serves 4

Ingredients:

1 cup brown lentils, cooked and drained

1 cup cherry tomatoes, halved

2 cucumbers, halved and thinly sliced

1/2 cup baby rocket leaves

1/2 red onion, finely cut

1 tbsp lemon juice

1 tsp honey

4 tbsp olive oil

6 oz haloumi, cut into slices

Directions:

Combine the lentils, tomatoes, cucumber, rocket leaves and onion in a salad bowl. Whisk together lemon juice, honey, olive oil, salt and pepper in a small bowl. Drizzle the dressing over the salad and toss to coat.

Pat the haloumi dry with a paper towel and toss in the remaining olive oil. Heat a frying pan over medium heat and cook the haloumi in batches, for one-two minutes each side or until golden. Transfer to a plate.

Divide the salad among serving plates. Top with haloumi and serve.

Brown Lentil Salad

Serves 4

Ingredients:

1 can lentils, drained and rinsed

1 red onion, thinly sliced

1 tomato, diced

1 red bell pepper, chopped

2 garlic cloves, crushed

2 tbsp lemon juice

1/3 cup parsley leaves

salt and pepper, to taste

Directions:

Place lentils, red onion, tomato, bell pepper and lemon juice in a large bowl.

Season with salt and black pepper to taste.

Toss to combine and sprinkle with parsley. Serve.

Baby Spinach Salad

Serves 4

Ingredients:

1 bag baby spinach, washed and dried

9 oz feta cheese, coarsely crumbled

1 red bell pepper, cut in slices

1 cup cherry tomatoes, cut in halves

1 red onion, finely chopped

1 cup black olives, pitted

1 tsp dried oregano

1 large garlic clove

3 tbsp red wine vinegar

4 tbsp olive oil

salt and freshly ground black pepper to taste

Directions:

Prepare the dressing by blending garlic and oregano with olive oil and vinegar in a food processor.

Place the spinach leaves in a large salad bowl and toss with the dressing. Add the rest of the ingredients and give everything a toss again. Season to taste with black pepper and salt.

Tabbouleh

Serves 6

Ingredients:

1 cup raw bulgur

2 cups boiling water

a bunch of parsley, finely cut

2 tomatoes, chopped

3 tbsp olive oil

2 garlic cloves, minced

6-7 fresh onions, chopped

1 tbsp fresh mint leaves, chopped

juice of two lemons

salt and black pepper

Directions:

Bring water and salt to a boil, then pour over bulgur. Cover and set aside for fifteen minutes to steam. Drain excess water from bulgur and fluff with a fork. Leave to chill.

In a large bowl, mix together the parsley, tomatoes, olive oil, garlic, green onions and mint. Stir in the chilled bulgur and season to taste with salt, pepper, and lemon juice.

Fatoush

Serves 6

Ingredients:

2 cups lettuce, washed, dried, and chopped

3 tomatoes, chopped

1 cucumber, peeled and chopped

1 green pepper, deseeded and chopped

1/2 cup radishes, sliced in half

1 small red onion, finely chopped

half a bunch of parsley, finely cut

2 tbsp finely chopped fresh mint

3 tbsp olive oil

4 tbsp lemon juice

salt and black pepper to taste

2 whole-wheat pita breads

Directions:

Toast the pita breads in a skillet until they are browned and crisp. Set aside.

Place the lettuce, tomatoes, cucumbers, green pepper, radishes, onion, parsley and mint in a salad bowl. Break up the toasted pita into bite-size pieces and add to the salad.

Make the dressing by whisking together the olive oil with the lemon juice, a pinch of salt, and some black pepper. Toss everything together until well coated with dressing and serve.

Greek Salad with Avocado

Serves 6

Ingredients:

2 cucumbers, diced

2 tomatoes, sliced

1 green lettuce, cut

2 red bell peppers, cut

1/2 cup olives, pitted

6 oz feta cheese, cubed

1 red onion, sliced

1 avocado, peeled and diced

2 tbsp olive oil

2 tbsp lemon juice

salt and ground black pepper, to taste

Directions:

Dice the cucumbers and slice the tomatoes. Tear the lettuce or cut it in thin strips. Deseed and cut the peppers in strips. Dice the avocado.

Mix all vegetables in a salad bowl. Add the olives and the feta cheese cut in cubes.

In a small cup mix the olive oil and the lemon juice with salt and pepper. Pour over the salad and stir again.

The Best Orzo Salad

Serves 6

Ingredients:

For the dressing:

1/3 cup extra-virgin olive oil

3/4 cup fresh lemon juice

1 tbsp dried mint

For the salad:

8 oz uncooked orzo

2 tbsp olive oil

a bunch of fresh onions, chopped

3 green peppers, diced

1/2 cup black olives, pitted, cut

2 tomatoes, diced

1 cup raw sunflower seeds

The dressing: Combine the olive oil, lemon juice, and mint in a small bowl, mixing well. Place the dressing in the refrigerator until ready to use.

Directions:

Cook the orzo according to package directions (in salted water) and rinse thoroughly with cold water when you strain it. Transfer to a large bowl and toss with the olive oil. Allow orzo to cool completely.

Once the orzo is cooled, add the diced peppers, finely cut fresh onions, olives and diced tomatoes stirring until mixed well.

Stir the dressing (it will have separated by this point) and add it to the salad, tossing to evenly coat. Add salt and pepper to taste and sprinkle with sunflower seeds.

Blue Cheese Iceberg Salad

Serves 6

Ingredients:

1 small iceberg salad

1 avocado, cut

1 cucumber, cut

1 red onion, cut

1/2 cup walnuts, raw

5.5 oz blue cheese, coarsely crumbled

¼ cup orange juice

3 tbsp olive oil

1 tbsp honey

salt

Directions:

Tear the iceberg lettuce or cut it in thin strips. Toss it in a medium salad bowl together with the other vegetables.

Add the coarsely crumbled blue cheese. Whisk together honey, orange juice, olive oil and salt and drizzle over the salad. Toss in the walnuts and serve.

Apple, Walnut and Radicchio Salad

Serves 4

Ingredients:

2 radicchio, trimmed, finely shredded

2 apples, quartered and thinly sliced

4 spring onions, chopped

1/2 cup walnuts, roasted

1 tbsp mustard

1 tbsp lemon juice

1/3 cup olive oil

Directions:

Prepare the dressing by combining mustard, lemon juice and olive oil.

Place walnuts on an oven tray and roast in a preheated to 400 F oven for three-four minutes or until brown.

Mix radicchio, apples, onions and walnuts in a large salad bowl. Add the dressing and toss to combine.

Apple, Celery and Walnut Salad

Serves 4

Ingredients:

4 apples, quartered, cores removed, thinly sliced

1 celery rib, thinly sliced

1/2 cup walnuts, chopped

2 tbsp raisins

1 large red onion, thinly sliced

3 tbsp apple cider vinegar

2 tbsp sunflower oil

Directions:

Mix vinegar, oil, salt and pepper in a small bowl. Whisk until well combined.

Combine apples, celery, walnuts, raisins and onion in a bigger salad bowl. Drizzle with dressing and toss gently.

Greek Chickpea Salad

Serves 4

Ingredients:

1 cup canned chickpeas, drained and rinsed

1 spring onion, finely cut

1 small cucumber, deseeded and diced

2 green bell peppers, diced

2 tomatoes, diced

2 tsp chopped fresh parsley

1 tsp capers, drained and rinsed

juice of half lemon

2 tbsp olive oil

1 tbsp balsamic vinegar

salt and pepper, to taste

a pinch of dried oregano

Directions:

In a medium bowl toss together the chickpeas, spring onion, cucumber, bell pepper, tomato, parsley, capers and lemon juice.

In a smaller bowl stir together the remaining ingredients and pour over the chickpea salad. Toss well to coat and allow to marinate, stirring occasionally, for at least 1 hour before serving.

Snow White Salad

Serves 4

Ingredients:

1 large or two small cucumbers -fresh or pickled

4 cups yogurt

1/2 cup of crushed walnuts

2-3 cloves garlic, crushed

1/2 bunch of dill

3 tbsp sunflower oil

salt, to taste

Directions:

Strain the yogurt in a piece of cheesecloth or a clean white dishtowel. You can suspend it over a bowl or the sink. Peel and dice the cucumbers, place in a large bowl.

Add the crushed walnuts and the crushed garlic, the oil and the finely chopped dill. Scoop the drained yogurt into the bowl and stir well.

Add salt to the taste, cover with cling film, and put in the fridge for at least an hour so the flavors can mix well.

Asian Coleslaw

Serves 4

Ingredients:

for the salad

1/2 Chinese cabbage, shredded

1 green bell pepper, sliced into thin strips

1 carrot, cut into thin strips

4 green onions, chopped

for the dressing

3 tbsp lemon juice

3 tbsp soy sauce

3 tbsp sweet chilly sauce

Directions:

Remove any damaged outer leaves and rinse cabbage. Holding cabbage from the base and starting at the opposite end shred leaves thinly.

Combine the vegetables in a salad bowl. Prepare the dressing by mixing lemon juice, soy sauce and sweet chilly sauce. Pour it over the salad and toss well.

Asian Carrot and Sprout Salad

Serves 4

Ingredients:

2 carrots, peeled and cut into ribbons

6 oz snow peas, trimmed, thinly sliced diagonally

2 cucumbers, cut into ribbons

1 cup bean sprouts, trimmed

1/2 cup snow pea sprouts, trimmed

1 tbsp sesame seeds, toasted

2 tbsp sunflower oil

2 tbsp rice wine vinegar

2 tsp sesame oil

1 tsp honey

Directions:

Mix sunflower oil, vinegar, sesame oil and honey and whisk to combine. Season with salt and pepper.

Put the carrot and snow peas in boiling water and let stand for two minutes or until snow peas turn bright green. Drain, rinse under cold water and place in a salad bowl.

Add in cucumber, beans sprouts, snow pea sprouts and sesame seeds. Drizzle with dressing, toss to combine and serve.

Shredded Egg Salad

Serves 4

Ingredients:

3 large hard boiled eggs, shredded

2-3 spring onions, finely cut

2-3 garlic cloves, crushed

4 tbsp homemade mayonnaise

1 tbsp mustard

1 tbsp yogurt

1 salt and pepper, to taste

Directions:

Peel the shell off of the eggs. Shred the eggs in a medium salad bowl.

Mix in the remaining ingredients. Serve chilled.

Fresh Greens Salad

Serves 8

Ingredients:

1 head red leaf lettuce, rinsed, dried and chopped

1 head green leaf lettuce, rinsed, dried, and chopped

1 head endive, rinsed, dried and chopped

1 cup frisee lettuce leaves, rinsed, dried, and chopped

3 leaves fresh basil, chopped

3-4 leaves fresh mint, chopped

4 tbsp olive oil

2 tbsp lemon juice

1 tbsp honey

salt, to taste

Directions:

Place the red and green leaf lettuce, frisee lettuce, endive, basil, and mint into a large salad bowl and toss lightly to combine.

Prepare the dressing from lemon juice, olive oil and honey and pour over the salad. Season with salt to taste.

Simple Broccoli Salad

Serves 4

Ingredients:

14 oz fresh broccoli, cut into florets

3-4 green onions, finely cut

1/3 cup raisins

1/3 cup sunflower seeds

1/2 cup yogurt

1/3 cup orange juice

1 tsp chia seeds

Directions:

Combine broccoli, onions, raisins, and sunflower seeds in a medium salad bowl.

In a smaller bowl, whisk together the yogurt, orange juice and chia seeds until blended. Pour over the broccoli mixture and toss to coat.

Caprese Salad

Serves 6

Ingredients:

4 tomatoes, sliced

5.5 oz mozzarella cheese, sliced

10 fresh basil leaves

3 tbsp olive oil

2 tbsp balsamic vinegar

salt to taste

Directions:

Slice the tomatoes and mozzarella, then layer the tomato slices, basil leaves and mozzarella slices on a plate.

Drizzle olive oil and balsamic vinegar over the salad and serve.

Bulgarian Green Salad

Serves 4

Ingredients:

1 green lettuce, washed and drained

1 cucumber, sliced

a bunch of radishes

a bunch of spring onions

juice of half lemon or 2 tbsp of white wine vinegar

3 tbsp olive oil

salt, to taste

Directions:

Cut the lettuce into thin strips. Slice the cucumber and the radishes as thinly as possible and chop the spring onions.

Mix all the salad ingredients in a large bowl, add the lemon juice and oil and season with salt to taste.

Green Superfood Salad

Serves 6

Ingredients:

4 cups mixed green salad leaves

2 cups broccoli or sunflower sprouts

1 avocado, cubed

2 cucumbers, chopped

1 tbs sunflower seeds

1 tbs pumpkin seeds

2 tbsp lemon juice

3 tbsp olive oil

1/2 tsp mustard

salt and pepper, to taste

Directions:

Mix all vegetables in a big salad bowl. Toss well to combine.

Prepare the dressing by whisking together olive oil, lemon juice and mustard.

Season with salt and pepper to taste. Drizzle over the salad and toss again.

Sprinkle the salad with sunflower and pumpkin seeds and serve.

Fried Zucchinis with Yogurt Sauce

Serves 4

Ingredients:

4 medium zucchinis

2 cups yogurt

3 cloves garlic, crushed

a bunch of fresh dill, chopped

1 cup sunflower oil

1 cup flour

salt

Directions:

Start by combining the garlic and chopped dill with the yogurt in a bowl. Add salt to taste and put in the fridge.

Wash and peel the zucchinis, and cut them in thin diagonal slices or in rings 1/4 in thick. Salt and leave them in a suitable bowl placing it inclined to drain away the juices.

Coat the zucchinis with flour, then fry turning on both sides until they are golden-brown (about 3 minutes on each side). Transfer to paper towels and pat dry.

Serve the zucchinis hot or cold, with the yogurt mixture on the side.

Cucumber Salad

Serves 4

Ingredients:

2 medium cucumbers, sliced

a bunch of fresh dill

1/2 tsp dried oregano

2 cloves garlic

3 tbsp white wine, vinegar

5 tbsp olive oil

salt to taste

Directions:

Cut the cucumbers in rings and put them in a salad bowl.

Add the finely cut dill, the pressed garlic and season with salt, oregano, vinegar and oil. Mix well and serve cold.

Tomato Couscous Salad

Serves 4

Ingredients:

7 oz medium couscous

1 cup hot water

2 ripe tomatoes, diced

1/2 red onion, finely cut

4 tbsp olive oil

4 tbsp lemon juice

1 tbsp dry mint

1 tsp chia seeds

Directions:

Place the couscous in a large bowl. Boil water with one tablespoon of olive oil and pour over the couscous.

Cover and set aside for ten minutes. Fluff couscous with a fork and when it is completely cold, stir in the tomatoes, onion and dry mint.

In a separate small bowl, combine the remaining olive oil, the lemon juice and salt, add to the couscous and stir until well combined.

Red Cabbage Salad

Serves 6

Ingredients:

1 small head red cabbage, cored and chopped

1 bunch of fresh dill, finely cut

3 tbsp sunflower oil

3 tbsp red wine vinegar

1 tsp sugar

2 tsp salt

black pepper, to taste

Directions:

In a bowl, mix the oil, red wine vinegar, sugar and black pepper. Place the cabbage in a large glass bowl. Sprinkle the salt on top and crunch it with your hands to soften.

Pour the dressing over the cabbage, and toss to coat. Sprinkle the salad with dill, cover it with foil, and leave in the refrigerator for half an hour before serving.

Cabbage, Carrot and Turnip Salad

Serves 4

Ingredients:

7 oz fresh white cabbage, shredded

7 oz carrots, shredded

7 oz white turnips, shredded

½ a bunch of parsley

2 tbsp white vinegar

3 tbsp sunflower oil

salt, to taste

Directions:

Combine first three ingredients need in a large bowl and mix well with hands.

Add salt, vinegar and oil. Stir and sprinkle with parsley. Set aside for 5 minutes, stir and serve

Carrot Salad

Serves 4

Ingredients:

4 carrots, shredded

1 apple, peeled, cored and shredded

2 garlic cloves, crushed

2 tbsp lemon juice

2 tbsp honey

salt and pepper to taste

Directions:

In a bowl, combine the shredded carrots, apple, lemon juice, honey, garlic, salt and pepper.

Toss to combine and chill before serving.

Bulgur Salad

Serves 4

Ingredients:

1 cup bulgur

2 cups boiling water

3 tablespoons olive oil

1/2 cup black olives, pitted, cut

1 tomato, chopped

2-3 fresh onions, finely cut

2 tbsp lemon zest

juice from two lemons

2 tbsp fresh mint, finely chopped

2 tbsp fresh parsley, finely chopped

salt and black pepper, to taste

Directions:

In a large salad bowl pour boiling water over bulgur. Stir in olive oil, lemon zest, lemon juice, mint and parsley and leave aside for thirty minutes.

Fluff bulgur with a fork and add the chopped tomato, onions and olives. Season with salt and pepper to taste and serve.

Roasted Eggplant and Pepper Salad

Serves 4

Ingredients:

2 medium eggplants

2 red or green bell peppers

2 tomatoes

3 cloves garlic, crushed

fresh parsley

1-2 tbsp red wine vinegar

olive oil, as needed

salt, pepper

Directions:

Wash and dry the vegetables. Prick the skin off the aubergines. Bake the aubergines, tomatoes and peppers in a pre-heated oven at 480 F for about forty minutes until the skins are well burnt.

Take out of the oven and leave in a covered container for about ten minutes. Peel the skins off and drain well the extra juices. Deseed the peppers.

Cut all the vegetables into small pieces. Add the garlic and mix well with a fork or in a food processor.

Add olive oil, vinegar and salt to taste. Stir again. Serve cold and sprinkled with parsley.

Shopska Salad

Serves 6

Ingredients:

3-4 tomatoes, diced

1 large cucumber, diced

1-2 fresh green peppers, cut

1 onion, chopped

5.5 oz feta cheese, grated

For the dressing:

4 tbsp apple cider vinegar

4 tbsp sunflower oil

salt to taste

To serve: 2-3 tablespoons of chopped flat-leaf parsley

Directions:

Cut the peppers into small strips and add the diced tomatoes, cucumbers and onion.

Add salt, oil, vinegar and mix. Serve topped with chopped parsley and grated feta cheese.

Okra Salad

Serves 4

Ingredients:

1.2 lb young okras

1 lemon

1/2 bunch parsley, chopped

2 hard tomatoes

3 tbsp sunflower oil

1/2 tsp black pepper

salt

Directions:

Trim okras, wash and cook in salted water. Drain and cool when tender. In a small bowl, mix well the lemon juice and sunflower oil, salt and pepper.

Pour over okras arranged in a bowl and sprinkle with chopped parsley. Wash tomatoes and cut them into slices, then garnish the salad with them.

Green Bean Salad

Serves 6

Ingredients:

2 cups green beans, cooked

1 onion, sliced

4 garlic cloves, crushed

1 tbsp fresh mint, chopped

1 bunch of fresh dill, finely chopped

3 tbsp olive oil

1 tbsp apple cider vinegar

salt and pepper to taste

Directions:

Pour the green beans in a medium bowl and mix with onion, mint and dill.

In a smaller bowl stir olive oil, vinegar, garlic, salt, and pepper. Toss into the green bean mixture.

Zucchini Pasta Salad

Serves 6

Ingredients:

2 cups whole wheat pasta

2 zucchinis, sliced and halved

4 tomatoes, cut

6 mushrooms, cut

1 small red onion, chopped

2 tbsp fresh basil, chopped

3.5 oz blue cheese

2 tbsp olive oil

1 tbsp lemon juice

black pepper, to taste

Directions:

Cook pasta according to package directions or until al dente.
Drain, rinse with cold water and drain again. Place zucchinis,
tomatoes, mushrooms and onion in large bowl. Add pasta and mix
gently.

Prepare a dressing by combining the olive oil, lemon juice, basil,
blue cheese and black pepper. Pour it over the salad. Toss gently
and serve.

Cheese Stuffed Tomatoes

Serves 4

Ingredients:

4 large tomatoes

9 oz feta cheese

1 tsp paprika

Directions:

Cut the top of each tomato in such a way as to be able to stuff the tomato and cover with the cap.

Scoop out the seeds and central part of the tomatoes to create a hollow. Mash the scooped out parts of the tomatoes, add to the feta cheese and stir to make a homogeneous mixture. Add paprika.

Stuff the tomatoes with the mixture and cover with the caps. Serve chilled, garnished with sprays of parsley.

Turkish Spinach Salad

Serves 1-2

Ingredients:

a few bunches of spinach stems

water to boil the stems

1 garlic clove, minced

lemon juice or vinegar, to taste

olive oil

salt, to taste

Directions:

Trim the stems so that they will remain intact. Wash the stems very well. Steam stems in a basket over boiling water for 2 to 3 minutes until wilted but not too fluffy.

Place them on a plate and sprinkle with minced garlic, olive oil, lemon juice or vinegar, and salt.

Bulgarian Spinach Salad

Serves 4

Ingredients:

1 bag baby spinach, washed and dried

4-5 spring onions, finely chopped

1 cucumber, cut

1/2 cup walnuts, halved

2/3 cup yogurt

3 tbsp red wine vinegar

4 tbsp olive oil

salt and freshly ground black pepper to taste

Directions:

Prepare the dressing by blending yogurt, olive oil and vinegar in a cup.

Place the spinach leaves in a large salad bowl together with the onions, cucumber and walnuts. Season to taste with black pepper and salt, stir well and toss with the dressing.

Green Bean and Rocket Salad with Green Olive Dressing

Serves 4

Ingredients:

7 oz green beans, cut into 1 in lengths

1/2 cup baby rocket leaves

green olive dressing

1/2 cup green olives, pitted, finely chopped

4 tbsp olive oil

1 tbsp balsamic vinegar

1 tsp mustard

salt and black pepper, to taste

Directions:

Prepare the dressing by combining chopped olives, olive oil, vinegar and mustard in a small bowl and whisking lightly. Season with salt and pepper to taste.

Cook the green beans in salted boiling water until bright green and tender crisp. Drain and rinse with cold water. Drain again.

Place rocket leaves and beans in a salad bowl. Drizzle with green olive dressing and toss to combine.

Mozzarella, Tomato and Basil Couscous Salad

Serves 4

Ingredients:

4 tomatoes, diced

1 cup fresh mozzarella cheese, diced

3-4 spring onions, very finely cut

2 tbsp olive oil

1 tbsp lemon juice

salt, to taste

1/4 teaspoon fresh ground black pepper

1 garlic clove, crushed

1 cup couscous

1 1/4 cups water

1/2 cup chopped fresh basil

Directions:

In a big salad bowl combine tomatoes, mozzarella, salt, pepper, garlic, lemon juice, olive oil and spring onions. Toss everything well, cover, and marinate for half an hour.

Boil the water and pour over the couscous. Set aside for five minutes then fluff with a fork. Add couscous to the tomato mixture along with the chopped basil leaves and toss again.

FREE BONUS RECIPES: 10 Natural Homemade Beauty Recipes that are Easy on the Budget

Dry Skin Body Scrub

Ingredients:

½ cup brown sugar

½ cup sea salt salt

2-3 tbsp honey

2 tbsp argan oil

2 tbsp fresh orange juice

Directions:

Mix all ingredients until you have a smooth paste. Apply to wet skin and exfoliate body in small, circular motions. Rinse with warm water.

Lavender Body Scrub Recipe

Ingredients:

1/2 cup sugar

2 tbsp lavender leaves

¼ cup jojoba oil

3 drops lavender essential oil

Directions:

Combine sugar and lavender leaves. Add jojoba oil and lavender essential oil. Apply the mixture to damp skin. Gently exfoliate in small, circular motions. Rinse with warm water.

Rosemary Body Scrub

Ingredients:

1/2 cup coconut oil

1/2 cup sugar

1/4 cup flax seeds

7-8 drops Rosemary Essential Oil

Directions:

Combine sugar and flax seeds and stir until mixed well. Add the coconut oil and mix until evenly combined. Apply the mixture to damp skin. Gently exfoliate in small, circular motions. Rinse with warm water.

Banana-Sugar Body Scrub

Ingredients:

1 ripe banana

4 tbsp raw sugar

1 tbsp cocoa powder

2 tbsp almond oil

¼ tsp pure vanilla extract

Directions:

Smash ingredients together with a fork. Gently massage over your body for a few minutes. Rinse off with warm water

Coffee Body Scrub

Ingredients:

1/4 cup ground coffee

1/4 cup sugar

3 tbsp olive oil

1 vitamin E capsule

Directions:

Mix sugar with ground coffee, olive oil and the Vitamin E capsule. Apply over wet body and massage gently. Rinse off with warm water.

Strained Yogurt Face Mask

Ingredients:

5 tbsp plain yogurt

1 slice of white bread

Directions:

This is a very old family recipe and is also the easiest basic face mask. It was used probably by every Bulgarian mother and grandmother back in the days when there were no commercial creams and moisturizers.

Place the slice of bread in a plate, put the yogurt on top of it, spread it evenly and leave in the fridge for a few hours or overnight. In the morning take the strained yogurt and spread it on your clean face, leave it for 20 minutes and rinse it with water. Results are always excellent.

Oats Bran Face Mask

Ingredients:

3 tbsp oats bran

hot water

2 drops Bulgarian rose essential oil

Directions:

Boil bran in 1/2 cup of water. Strain, cool, add rose oil and apply to face. Leave for 15 minutes and wash with lukewarm water.

Pear and Honey Mask

Ingredients:

1 ripe pear

1 tbsp honey

1 tsp sour cream

Directions:

Peel and cut the pear, then mash it with a fork into a smooth paste. Stir in a tablespoon of honey and a teaspoon of cream.

Spread the mixture evenly over your face and neck. Leave it for 10 minutes then rinse off.

Banana Nourishing Mask

Ingredients:

1 banana

1 tsp honey

1 tsp plain yogurt

Directions:

Mash a banana, add the honey and the yogurt, mix well and spread it evenly on a clean face. Leave it for at least 15 minutes and wash with cold water.

Apple Autumn Mask

Ingredients:

1/2 apple

1 tsp oatmeal

1 tsp honey

Directions:

Take a ripe half apple, grate it and mash it with a fork. Add one teaspoon oatmeal and one teaspoon honey to it and stir well.

Spread on face and leave it on until the mixture dries completely then rinse it off with ordinary water.

About the Author

Vesela lives in Bulgaria with her family of six (including the Jack Russell Terrier). Her passion is going green in everyday life and she loves to prepare homemade cosmetic and beauty products for all her family and friends.

Vesela has been publishing her cookbooks for over a year now. If you want to see other healthy family recipes that she has published, together with some natural beauty books, you can check out her Author Page on Amazon.